Bicycles

Chris Oxlade

Heinemann Library
Chicago, Illinois

Designed by Paul Davies and Associates
Originated by Ambassador Litho Ltd
Printed in Hong Kong, China

05 04 03 02 01
10 9 8 7 6 5 4 3 2 1

Library of Congress Cataloging-in-Publication Data
 Oxlade, Chris.
      Bicycles / Chris Oxlade.
              p. cm. – (Transportation around the world)
      Includes bibliographical references and index.
      Summary: Describes the early development of bicycles, different kinds of bikes,
and how they are used.
      ISBN 1-57572-300-X (lib.)
      1. Bicycles—Juvenile literature. [1. Bicycles and bicycling.] I. Title. II. Series.

TL412 .O95 2000
629.227'2—dc21
                                                                    00-025764

Acknowledgments
The publisher would like to thank the following for permission to reproduce photographs:
Allsport/Frank Baron, p.16; David Cannon, p. 17; Corbis/Karl Weatherly, p. 6; Hulton-Deutsch Collection, pp. 8, 9; Bettmann, p. 10; Phil Schermeister, p. 20; Galen Rowell, p. 22; Peter Turnley, p. 24; Earl Kowall, p. 25; The Stock Market/Paul Barton, p. 4; Charles Gupton, p. 5; Tony Stone Images–Hulton Getty, p. 10; Chris Shinn, p. 12; Lori Adamski Peek, p. 13; Greg Adams, p. 14; Jean-Marc Truchet, p. 28; Trip/J. Ringland, pp. 18, 19; S. Grant, p. 23; T. Freeman, p. 26; G. Contorakes, p. 27; G. Howe, p. 29.

Cover photo: Tony Stone

Every effort has been made to contact copyright holders of any material reproduced in this book. Any omissions will be rectified in subsequent printings if notice is given to the publisher.

Note to the Reader
Some words are shown in bold, **like this.**
You can find out what they mean by looking in the glossary.

Contents

What Is a Bicycle?

A bicycle is a machine that moves on two wheels. People use bicycles to go to work or school, or just for fun. The rider sits on a seat called a saddle and pushes **pedals** to move.

Balancing on a bicycle can be hard at first. This child's bike has two small extra wheels called training wheels. They keep the bicycle from falling over.

How Bicycles Work

A rider makes a bicycle move by turning the **pedals** with his or her feet. The pedals pull a **chain,** and the chain makes the back wheel go around.

Brakes make a bicycle slow down. To
work one kind of brakes, a rider squeezes
a **lever** on the handlebar. This makes
rubber pads press against the wheel.

The First Bicycles

The first bicycles were called hobbyhorses. They did not have **pedals**. Instead, the rider pushed against the ground to move the hobbyhorse along.

These bicycles were made about 100 years ago. They have pedals and **chains,** like bicycles today, and **rubber** tires on their wheels, too.

High-Wheelers

This bicycle is called a high-wheeler, or penny-farthing. It was first made in about 1870. Its name comes from the names of two old British coins.

The **pedals** of a high-wheeler are on the big front wheel. The rider sits on a saddle above the wheel. Getting on and off is very hard.

Where Are Bicycles Used?

In China, millions of people travel to and from work on their bicycles. Not many people have cars. City roads are filled with bicycle riders.

Some bicycles can travel on bumpy dirt paths. People use these kinds of bicycles to go into the countryside or up hills and mountains.

Mountain Bikes

A mountain bike is used for riding over rough, muddy, or hilly ground. This rider is wearing a helmet in case she falls off.

Tires with a large **tread** keep the bike from slipping on muddy ground. The **suspension** lets the wheels move up and down as the bicycle goes over bumps.

Racing bikes

Cyclists race against each other on roads or cycle tracks. They ride special racing bikes that can travel as fast as a car on a city street.

Some racing cycles have solid **frames** and wheels. These help the cycle go faster. The rider wears a special smooth helmet.

frame

solid wheel

Trick Bikes

Riders can perform many trick moves on bicycles called BMX bikes. Riders go from side to side along a **half-pipe**, doing spins and **somersaults**.

18

Kids and young adults
throughout the world
ride BMX bikes for fun
and in contests.
Spins, hops, and
wheelies are some of
the most exciting tricks.

rod

Recumbent Bikes

This strange looking bike is called a recumbent bicycle. The rider lies back in a seat instead of sitting up.

Since the rider sits in a comfortable position, he or she can ride for a long time. The special design helps a recumbent bike go faster than other bikes.

Touring Bikes

People who go on long journeys by bicycle use special touring bicycles. These bicycles are good for cycling on hard, smooth roads.

Traveling **cyclists** must carry camping supplies and extra clothes. These things are put in bags called panniers. Panniers are attached to the bike to make riding easier.

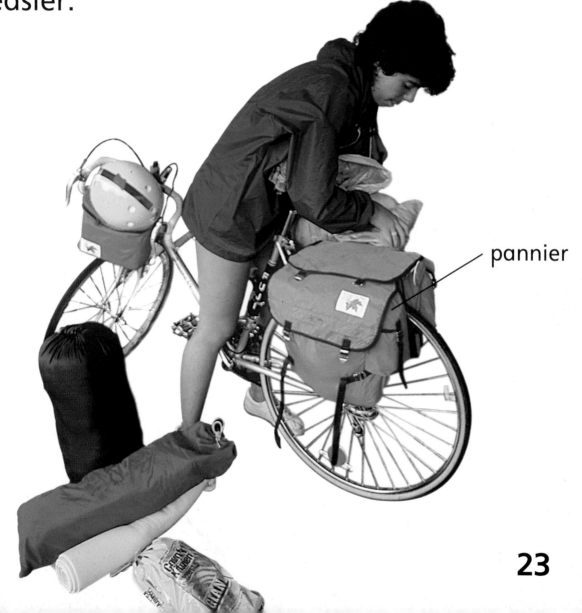

pannier

Rickshaws

In some countries, like India, people use rickshaws instead of taxis. Rickshaws move quickly and easily through busy city streets.

Some rickshaws have a hood to cover the seats in case of rain. Rickshaws often have colorful pictures and decorations on the seats, hoods, and handlebars.

Tandems

A tandem is a bicycle for two people to ride. It has two saddles and two sets of handlebars. Two people can have fun riding together.

A tandem also has two pairs of **pedals**, one for each rider. They are joined together by a **chain**. Tandem bikes can go very fast because two people are pedaling.

Unicycles

A unicycle has only one wheel. The rider has to keep pedaling to move and to stay balanced. On a unicycle, the rider can **pedal** backward or forward.

Many people all over the world enjoy watching performers on unicycles. Some circus performers use unicycles in their shows while juggling and doing other tricks.

Important Dates

1700s The first type of bicycle is called a hobbyhorse. It has no **pedals** or brakes.

1865 The first bicycle with pedals appears.

1870 The first high-wheeler bicycle appears. It has a big front wheel and a tiny back wheel.

1874 A type of bicycle called a safety bicycle is invented. It has a **chain** and brakes, and looks like a modern bicycle.

1888 John Dunlop invents a bicycle tire filled with air called a pneumatic tire. Before this, tires were made with solid **rubber**.

1903 Cyclists set out on the first *Tour de France* cycle race. The race is about 2,500 miles (4,000 kilometers) long and takes 23 days to finish, with a race on each day.

Glossary

chain   loop made of metal pieces that connects a bicycle's pedals to its back wheel

cyclist   person who rides a bicycle

frame   main piece of a bicycle that all the other parts are attached to, usually made of metal tubes joined together

half-pipe   special track for trick bicycles that has round slopes on each side, like a tube cut in two

lever   bar that moves and causes something to happen

pedal   part of the bicycle the rider pushes with his or her feet to make the bicycle move

rubber   soft, bouncy material that is used to make tires and brake pads on bicycles

somersault   trick move in which a rider goes head over heels and lands back on the wheels

steering   guiding which way the bicycle is going

suspension   part of the bicycle that connects the wheels to the rest of the bicycle

tread   part of the tire that touches the road

wheelie   bicycle trick in which a rider balances on the back wheel with the front wheel in the air

Index

More Books to Read

Richards, Brant. *Fantastic Book of Mountain Biking.* Brookfield Conn.: Millbrook Press, Incorporated, 1998.

Schaefer, Lola. *Bicycles.* Mankato, Minn.: Capstone Press, 1999.